G000060585

Where Is
My Parade?

Revisited

Poems, Short Stories, and Thoughts

Includes select poems from "Where is My Parade?"

By Carla Janell Lawson "Isis The Poet"

Published by CJL Books

U.S. Copyright 1-11999065411
ISBN: 978-1-0881-1873-3

Acknowledgments

I would like to- no, I must, acknowledge the following: God, Greta Freightman, Andrew Lawson-Freightman, Corey Lawson, Ola Lawson, Judy Hall, Valerie Williams, Bennye Blackman, Pattsy Blackman, Flossie Weir, Andrew Thompson, Lisa Mills Washington, Nicole Forrest, Donna Collins, Natashia Grant, Arthur Roland, Archie Thompson, Michelle Williams, Tamie Griffin, Bruce and Sharisse Taylor, Ryan Cerami, Valerie Oakley, Erma Smit,h and Linda Pinkney. All of whom helped me to push through the most devastating experience of my life, the transition of my mother Jennifer Blackman. Your support and love, however it was given in any form, whether you knew it or not, was critically formidable during my healing process which is still ongoing. I will never forget any contributions people make to my life and all of you have been consistent, gracious and inspirational.

Shawn William and Toni Blackman, to say thank you would be a significant understatement. While struggling through deep pain and grief the two of you insisted that I be aware of my capacity as an artist/writer. You called, called me on my shit, offered support, encouragement, a listening ear, constructive criticism all while being kind, loving, empathetic and insistent that I stretch, grow and push myself to get out of the box and represent my greatest self. You may never know how valuable and appreciated what you gave me at the time that I needed it most- will always be to me.

Dedication

I dedicate this book to myself, Carla Janell Lawson.
Because this one is for me.

True love

He was hand carved from a tree in Heaven
Just for me
He was no daydreaming fantasy
This was real and couldn't get any better

When I was draped in his arms the Sun smiled
The Moon grew full
The Stars shone brighter
Time
Stopped for us

I worried not about humanly flaws
To me he was perfect
I exposed myself to my very core
No one but God himself knew me better

You have to understand that he was Moses
And I was the Red Sea
I parted for him

This was love at its fullest
Early morning and late-night sleepy loving
Blinded me into unbreakable hypnosis

Strong hands touched every inch of me
In places that I thought untouchable
Not a moment passed where we weren't connected
We held conversational Tango
Without a word spoken

He had become a part of me
I was becoming more of him
We were becoming
Us
Completed by the thought of it
In agreement without doubt about it

This was no handheld walk in the park
This was an embrace shared
As we canvassed universal planes
Together
Tickled and tantalized
He had me stuttering
Unrecognizable sounds escaped my mouth
When I had words
I was still speechless

He took my breath away
And then gave it back to me
Fresh and new

I felt seduced and sedated by the savior in him
He was my ebony warrior king
I was first queen Isis
All over again

We didn't worry about tomorrow
Because out todays never ended
Spectacular and delicious
This science we'd mastered
To the point where nothing else mattered

This was not a real life fantasy
This was real life love
At its fullest

This right here
What we had
Was true love

I want to give you an everlasting love...

-Chaka Khan-

Apology to My Womb

In searching for an elusive connection
What I should have shared sparingly
Was given away freely
I allowed thieves and trespassers
To have access to my womb
And for this
To the most precious part of my person
I apologize

I apologize to my womb for being selfish
Deluded by lust
And easily persuaded
By fractures of attention and affection

I opened my legs one time too many
Allowing the unworthy to hide in a Holy Place
That I was entrusted in this body
To guard and protect

With wanton abandon
I have held onto shoulders
Clawed muscled backs
Begging for more

Of course without hesitation
I was obliged
With deep pounding
And reckless penetration
That caused massive spiritual contusions
With serious psychological ramifications
Complete with the manifestations of confusion
And for these womb intrusions
To the most precious part of my person
I apologize

I apologize to my womb
For the assaults that I personally aggravated
Trying to reach a higher level of pleasure
By giving complete and full access
To my Divine Center away

I pleaded for terrorists diguised as lovers
To stay inside of me
Overlooking
Dismissing
That there was no love involved
In our lovemaking

I allowed my womb to be used by outsiders
For games of conquer and divide
King of the Mountain
And
Who's your daddy
Only to end up with the same results
Time and time again

Depleted empty and alone
I was left with the taste of salty sweat
False promises
And an absence of tenderness
While my womb cried out continually for repair
From years of misappropriated trust
And bordered on irreparable damage
For this
To the most precious part of my person
I apologize

I apologize with deepest regrets and all sincerity
To my womb
I apologize for not treating you
Like the Sacred Garden that you are

I am so very sorry
For the garbage
That I allowed to take up residence
In your harbor
For giving penile assassins a map
To your treasures
I shamefully admit that I have failed you
I have nothing to show
For the pilgrimages made in your name

My only recourse at this point is to rebuild
Nurture and strengthen you
With every breath that I take

I hereby make a vow of commitment to you

I vow to love you
with the same fire and intensity as the Sun
in an effort to heal you

I vow to cherish, honor and protect you
With the same fierceness
That I used to cherish, honor and protect
Those that I allowed to help destroy
The power that you represent

I vow to consider your process
And process with consideration
Your purpose and plight
At all times

Lastly
I vow never again
To allow you to be treated like an escape route
Emergency exit
Sleeping pill

Sedative or pillow
For anyone else
For as long as I shall live

Damn
I apologize
I apologize to the most precious part of my person
For an adult lifetime
Of betrayal, molestation and deceit

Please
Forgive me

We Started As Queens

We started as Queens
Royal, Regal, Ravishingly beautiful Rulers of Great lands
We did that

Fierce, Fearless, Confidants and counterparts to Kings
Gave birth to Warriors, Scholars, Nations- Noah, Solomon,
Jesus Christ
We started as Queens

Trusted, respected, appreciated and admired
prayerful, loyal, compassionate and empathetic
Back straight, head high, eyes clear and direct
integrity and morals intact
We Started as Queens
NEFERTARI

And they all wanted us
from any and every land
upon sight they wanted us
for miles and miles
the men would fight because they wanted us

We supported our sisters
we were protected by our brothers
we respected our elders
my children were her children
her children were my children
we would've died for them
we weren't afraid of our children

and the penalty for treason
was death
We Started as Queens
ISIS

But one day the boats came
shipload by shipload
we were stolen and transplanted
displaced and disgraced
They stole enough of us to build this nation
underestimating the fact that a forced migration
could not extinguish the power of royal DNA
They did not know that for a queen to rule
she does not need a literal throne
That through cultural and spiritual assassinations
she will always have something in her that surpasses
imposed limitations
because
We Started as Queens
CLEOPATRA

transition
slavery to Jim Crow
our ancestors had to teach us to harness our power
to suppress our voices,
so we could survive a time in history
where the fear of our capabilities as Queens could cost us our
lives

transition
Jim Crow to the black Power Revolution
our elders fought to reclaim our status
to erase the persona non grata that we had been granted
They died for us to be recognized for who we were
because they had not forgotten that
We Started as Queens
NZINGHA

Transition
we went from genocide to suicide
we went from being sold
to selling out

to selling one another
And somewhere there is a tomb of queens whose ashes have turned to tears
because they have great -great- great granddaughters who don't know who they are
they do not know where they are from
they do not know what they represent
they don't even know their own names
they respond to "come here bitch" (catcalls) and insults
they conform to being a side piece
they videotape beating one another senseless, mercilessly
they buy ass and breasts like we bought Nikes and starter jackets
their claim to social fame is high priced shoes and bags
and we just wanted to go to college
They have no common sense, wisdom and even less knowledge
Something is wrong with this picture
We Started as Queens
MEKADA

The change has to begin somewhere and the time is now
you cannot break down what is already broken
this season is for building
for refilling, regenerating, revitalizing and energizing
for nurturing and teaching
for sowing and reaching
OUT
to the young women in our lives
our daughters cannot be on a first name basis with us
teach them respect
our daughters cannot curse, drink, or smoke with us
teach them respect
our daughters cannot have grown men spend the night in our homes with us
teach them respect
our daughters cannot leave home with any body parts meant

to be covered by underwear exposed
teach them to respect themselves
They need boundaries, morals, standards, role models that
look like them
some of them just need a hug
and some of them need a good slap in the mouth
do whatever it takes
teach them integrity by doing what you say
and saying what you mean
We can start breaking chains by telling them every day
We Started as Queens
YAA ASANTEWA

When I reach for my pen, I have to scrape it against my scars to write.- Maya Angelou

When I wake up, no make-up, half naked, I feel like I'm the shit...

Sa-Roc

Haiku #1

When I'm real hungry

I feast on the thought of you

To only want more

What I want

I want a love that's more like cake than icing

A man that's more like God than other men

A spirit more like mine than yours

A song about me instead of money

A day for living instead of being alive

A time for romance instead of movies

A hand for holding instead of shoving

A pen that never runs out of ink

A notebook with self-generating pages

A meal that's orgasmic instead of filling

A smile that's genuine instead of conditional

A friend that's strangely unique

A rainbow that doesn't fade

Colors that multiply and expand into more colors

I want someone to love me

Just like I am

Because I am

Who I am

That's what I want

The mind objector, heart protector, sole defender of anything I feel....

Heather Headley

Protection

When I look into the eyes of little brown girls
I see the absence of dreams
I see the excess of insanity
Where there was once a light
There is now a dark abyss

They carry iPhones,Ipads and babies
Like we used to carry
Jump ropes and babydolls

They process adult thoughts in little girl minds
Wear grown women's clothes
On well developed little girl bodies
They are stressed out in elementary school
Pregnant in junior high
Suicidal or homicidal in high school

They have wounds
These little brown girls
Cuts and extensive abrasions
That never seem to go away
Due to consistent exposure
To contaminated environments
That are inclusive of
Verbal assaults
Emotional jabs
Mental haymakers that paralyze and fester

They long to be little girls freely
To have few fears and worries
But their bodies betray them
And bring about womanly concerns

They would rather be laughing and loving openly
But their surroundings betray them

Enveloping them in arenas of negativity
Rejection and apathy

Where there should be ponytails and ribbons
There are clouds of confusion
Where there should be hugs and kisses
There are burdens and responsibilities
Where there should be protection
There is exposure
To
Strange hands
Penetration
Subliminal messages that say
You are not enough
You should look like someone else
You are not enough
You should be like someone else
You are not enough
You won't
You can't
You shouldn't
You are not
Enough

The eyes that should have dreams in them hold tears
The heads that should be held up high
Are hanging low
The feet that should be skipping rope
Are shuffling
The minds that should be full of vigor, life, and desire
Are boggled, heavy and misunderstood
The spirits that should be soaring
Are broken

These little brown girls
Wounded, scorned, broken and empty
Become brown women

Wounded, scorned, broken and empty
What was once fertile ground in a precious vessel
Is now a barren plateau
Encompassed in something
Cracked, torn and tarnished

As women
These damaged little girls hide in plain sight
They smile with daggers in their eyes
Laugh with vinegar on their lips
And love with malice in their hearts
Desperately seeking
Hoping
That someone will come and love the pain away

They disappear in lovemaking bliss
Becoming the passion that consumes them
Wanting nothing more
Than to just feel
Whole and alive
Without having to participate
In a life that holds memories

Memories that hurt and burn
Memories that feel
Like mirrors in a funhouse
Strange and distorted

What they are looking for
These women
Is a smile that soothes the burns
Hands that melt the pain
Minds that consider the process
But don't process the consideration
A love that yields

Grows and covers

So that the mornings aren't so rude
The nights aren't so long
The unbearable is less cumbersome

Who I ask you
Is going to show up for them
The little brown girls
Turned brown women
To make their protection
A priority
Where is
Their protection

Tales of a little Black Girl - #1

I remember when I wanted *them* all to like me so very much. I was tired of being "different". I was hurt from the name calling and being chased home from school. *They* seemed to enjoy my fear and my hurt. So, I put a spell on *them* to make *them* love me. And then we grew up, and a lot of *them* did. I really wish I hadn't done that. Because *they* are *still* not my people.

If I didn't define myself for myself, I would be crunched into other people's fantasies for me and eaten alive. - Audre Lorde

Ain't it funny how the way you feel, shows on your face....

Earth Wind and Fire

A Mother's Heart

I did not know love until I met my son

I just thought I did

I didn't know that I could ever

love anyone as deeply and unconditionally as I do him

I had never met anyone that I would die for

And I had never met anyone who made me want to live

He was seven when I met him

Wearing spiderman pajama pants and an incredible hulk t-shirt

We made eye contact and fell in love

He went from holding my leg and looking up at me

To standing by my side and asking questions while looking into my eyes

And now

He stands over me and looks down while telling me about his day

I tried my best to teach him everything that I could think of about life

I wanted him to be equipped for everything

and anyone

I did not lie to him, sugar coat nor hold back anything

Even when his eyes clearly said "why are you telling me this?"

I kept feeding him love and information

But I always wonder, as I assume most parents do

Did I give him enough

Did I give him enough

to survive in a world that may not respect him

Have I taught him the rules of war properly

Will he be able to maneuver if and when he is stopped or approached by someone

Who doesn't see my baby when they see him

They see a 6 ft tall 300 lb problem

Will they see the innocence in his 18-year-old sheltered eyes

Will they suspect that he's still a baby

or will they see my baby as a suspect

He doesn't know what hatred feels like

He has never encountered a life-or-death situation

He doesn't understand why some people will immediately see him as threat

Because of his size

and

the color of his skin

He has never had to worry about defending himself against strangers

Whether it be physically or verbally

The only courtroom he's ever seen was the one we signed adoption papers in

Every time he leaves my house I pray

I pray for mercy, grace, his safety and return

And I pray that I never have to go to the penitentiary

Because somebody was fucking with my son

And they didn't know

that at the moment they became a problem for him

That I became a major problem for them

Please don't touch him

I followed the manual

He is respectful, kind, honest, hardworking and straightforward

He is sometimes shy, has a great sense of humor and all he wants to do currently

Is master his ps5 and get through college

Which I encourage

Yet and still

It needs to be understood that I still see my baby

But the reality is that he is a Black man in America

A country that loves to hate him

A place that will emasculate and regurgitate him

A place that has the capacity to shackle him with paperwork

And string him up by his feet with words like

Fit the profile

Threatening

Aggressive

Probable cause

Self defense

So I greet him every morning with I love you

I fill him every day with solutions to

scenarios and possible situations

And before he goes to sleep at night

I check on my man child

I make sure that nothing that happened during his day

Robbed or stripped him of his manhood in any way

Because I know

I know that with all of the good that I put in him

With all of the love that I gave him

And with all of the wisdom and knowledge that I share with him

One day

It may not be enough

But at the least I want him

To have a fighting chance

Divine Remembrance

I saw a face and was reminded of a place
that in this life I had not been-
through divine remembrance I felt the fire of a past life's love
even though in this life we would only be friends

I remember you King- that's why I know you so well
I know it puzzles you when I read your mind or understand
the stories that you tell
I remember you and being loved by you
in a place where there's no space or time
a friendship in this life is not a loss
because through spirits once connected
Love did not go blind

It saw through the eye of the soul and sought to redefine
Thanks to divine remembrance
in some way or another you'll always be mine
I am grateful for our reunion and the chance to love you
again
Even though in this body all we will be is friends

I'm still the Queen that rose with you and never left your side
I'm still the love you needed
The one who held you up when you cried
You may not see it, may never know it
Your memory may not provide
The elation of past sensations that still in my mind reside

Simple conversation invites deep understanding
as our paths become intertwined again
And even though I remember a passion beyond
comprehension
I will honor the path laid out for us
the gift of having you as a friend

I'll keep a promise made long ago

I'll still love you until life's end
That's the beauty of divine remembrance
It awakens the heart and stirs the soul
It took me to a place where I was the half that made you whole
Where nothing could touch or shake
What we'd built together
And now spirits reconnected as friends
Have afforded us another forever
I remember you King
I remember

I'm young and I'm old, I'm rich and I'm poor, feels like I've been on this Earth, many times before...

Teena Marie

Sick

Excuses for apathy
Rationalizations for abuse
Pedophiles clothed in couture
desecration of baby girls so common we are almost used
To it

It being the unspoken, the avoided, the swept under the rug
Atrocities of low life high paid virtue stealing thugs
There are no walls that can be built to protect our little girls
They are subject to scrutiny and contempt every time they are
Violated in this fucked up system we call our world
We sick boss

Sick and tired of being sick and tired
How dare you talk about supporting one other
while giving a monster a pass
and then attack the parents or question the ethics and
judgement
of a child
A child with breasts she isn't prepared to carry
Hips she doesn't know the meaning of
And an ass that she thinks is for leggings

The perpetual cycle of no self- love
Climbs at a cataclysmic rate
These little girls in women's bodies
become victims to men
who actually hate Women

The attraction is baffling, and then there are the predecessors
to current predators
Whose roots are intertwined in history that no one wants to
admit
That this is not new shit
Uncles, cousins, daddies, brothers and boyfriends

Stepfathers, grandfathers, the neighbor, pastor and the
policeman
Molesting bodies, assassinating spirits, breeding contempt
and self- hatred
And getting away with it
We sick boss

Make a statement on social media
Apologize
speak of the willingness of all involved
To be involved
avoid the dialogue about a child with adult appearance is still
a child none the
less
She is unable to comprehend the depth of damage that you do
to her
She has no idea
how your actions will impact her critical thinking skills for
the rest of her life
She doesn't even know that you should have no interest in
her
That your only interest in her is not of interest
It is sheer lust
Your only desire for her is dominance
No substance or goals of lifetime care full of love and growth
with guidance

She is an outlet for you and your craving for something
untouched that you can master
And devour
a notch in your belt
feather in your cap
that you can turn into a robot who squeals for your pleasure
All the while as your actions are revealed
the public is actually taking sides
about who is at fault
We sick boss

I would like to apologize
for the curse that you must be living under
As the daughter of a black man who would've killed you
with his bare hands
For just the thought of it
It being the violation and mind-bending manipulation that
you called mutual consent
I apologize

I am so very sorry
that no one has made it a point
to allow you
to mutually consent
to being their little girl
for a little while

Would you be okay with a little pee and a few threesomes
with people of the same gender
Or is that reserved for recipients with good behavior
Can you explain to me how a girl can turn you on
Make you excited about her body enough to forfeit your
integrity
Put your manhood into a questionable box

What did she say
that was so mind blowing and sexy
That you couldn't help yourself
Remembering 14
I just can't imagine what could've been exchanged verbally
that didn't
Sound an alarm in your head that said hell naw

But maybe you don't have a no button
Maybe you are the untouchable
capable of the unimaginable
doing the unthinkable
To our little girls

with no accountability
or legal ramifications
while maintaining your public status
We sick boss

I hope that you don't feel ostracized or attacked
Singled out or discriminated against
Be advised that you are not alone
We despise all of you
That entire body of sickness and depravity
Residing in males and females alike
I believe it was once said
We are legions
While there will be understanding that you are ill
There will be no empathy for ill bread actions

Fractions and splinters of young women
have been distributed into mainstream society
courtesy of the likes of you
I hope you get the help that you need
A therapist
a jail cell
or perhaps a 16-year drug induced coma

That seems to be your number
After decades of debauchery
Centuries of desecration- your actions preceded you
It seems like you're ready
You and many others
To go all the way
To hell
Now
If we can just get past a system
that allows a man who has intercourse with a 6-month-old
Babygirl to go free
we might be alright
one day
Damn
We sick boss

Don't Forget

The mass hysteria currently holding the title of government
in the country we reside in
is set up to make us forget
Don't forget
To keep us in a dark and sunken place, cloudy and
misguided- unsure of what to do or how
Don't forget-

They fear us remembering so they explode from spontaneous
desperation
 afraid we might have aspirations of affirmation
 for education and assimilation
 as a people we hold all of the power but live in its shadow.
Don't forget

We live in a country where the President can grab you by the
pussy
Black babies get shot for having toys
Black Boys get shot for having candy and cell phones
Black girls are found dead in hotel freezers
Black women are dying of "apparent suicides"
Black elders are dragged from vehicles and homes with no
respect or empathy for physical limitations
Don't you dare forget

Call the police- they're walking
Call the police- they're talking
Call the police - they're barbecuing
Call the police- they're swimming
Call the police- they're sitting in a car
Call the police- they're shopping
Call the police- they're eating
Call the police- they're selling water
Call the police- they're existing
Call the police-
They are Black

Call the police- they'll go to jail
Call the police
They'll kill them
Don't forget

Don't forget who you are
That you are the most emulated people on the planet
While simultaneously being the most disrespected
Don't forget that you naturally drip regality
That you are drenched in historic gold
That you reek of substance and strength so mighty
That they want everything that you have

They want your clothes
Your language
Your music
Your hair
Your men
Your women and your children
They want to look like you
To sound like you
To dance like you
They want to cook your food
And eat what you eat
Some of them even want your story and your skin
But they could never handle the assignment that comes with
any of it
They want to be you without paying the price

So no
Don't you forget
who you are
The descendants of royalty and revolutionaries
Of masters and innovators
The people who were created in Gods own image
Laced with skin in a rainbow of shades of cocoa
Hair so glorious that it comes to life

A spirit so mighty that it owns several continents
The people cut from a warriors cloth and engineering genius

And you have the audacity to bow down
To not fight,
To not vote
To refuse to acknowledge being of African descent
To glorify modern day minstrel on reality shows
To be afraid of your own children
To disrespect one another on global platforms
Niggas ain't shit and these hoes ain't loyal

Black people can't be mentally ill or hurt or damaged
Conditioned to manage a life while feeling nothing
And no one would understand anyway
400 years of physical and systemic oppression
Dying at the hands of predators with credentials
And then we kill each other for sport

It is all so very sick and maddening
But everything will be just fine you know
Because all we need is Jesus and an ass whooping
I promise you this is the real shit
So don't you forget
Don't you dare forget
Or you will look around one day
And everything will be the same shade of beige
And you'll find yourself struggling
Trying to remember
Don't forget

Remember who checks on you when you
get a little quiet- those are your people.-
Author Unknown

This is America, Don't catch you slippin now, Look what I'm whipping now...

Childish Gambino

Haiku #2

Blacks in this country
Like diamonds in Africa
Stay covered in blood

Kiss

You kissed me and I was awakened
A fire left to dwindle now rekindled
There was no way to tell you
what it was to me
how I felt
Knowing who you were
how you could possibly be
everything I had longed for
wanted
Needed
Desired
I was full from the thought of you
Wishing, wondering, questioning
How you came along at
The right
Wrong time
Making me crave you
Hunger for you
Resisting the urge to
move with reckless abandon
Join you
Stand by your side
And love you
Fearlessly
All because of a kiss
that touched my soul
and opened closed doors
Forcing me to
Remember

Tales of a little black girl #2

He was blue black, blacker than me. Always calling me a Black ass something, or an African booty scratcher. Trying to make me feel like something was wrong with my Black.

I saw him not long ago. He's still blue black, blacker than me. He's married to high yella girl with rashes. All I could think was- Who's the African booty scratcher now?

Karma is not created by thoughts or deeds; it is created by the intention behind the deed. -Author Unknown

Hey Sista, Soul Sista!

Angie Stone

Song of Solomon

8 We have a little sister, and she hath no breasts,
What shall we do for our sister in the day that she shall be
spoken for
9 If she be a wall- we will build upon her a palace of silver
And if she be a door we will enclose her with boards of
Cedar.
Song of Solomon 8: 8-9

For the round table discussions about my little sisters'
imperfections
I pray for forgiveness
For the snickers and giggles that burst forth
Without compassion or sensitivity
When I saw the nappy hair
Outdated or ill fitted clothing
Overrun shoes
Poor color choices for cosmetics
And bad grammar
I pray for mercy

For the time I did not take to offer my little sisters support
Encouragement, advice, knowledge, wisdom
Or a probably much needed hug
I pray for guidance and discernment

For all of the love that I shared
With inconsiderate, ungrateful, selfish
Apathetic women
Who live in a world boxed in mayhem
I pray for more love
I pray for more love so that I always have enough in my heart
To coat and ease the pain
Of my sisters who have never been reached out to

May I always take into consideration

That there was once a time
When my makeup was too bright and too heavy
There was a time when my hair was just plain wrong
My clothes too tight
My language filthy and inappropriate
My motives for action
Or lack thereof
Were selfish and lacking in humility

May I always remember that there were women
My older sisters
Who did not find my flaws as comical or weaknesses
They only saw them
As unnecessary
For my older sisters who enclosed my door
With boards of Cedar
I pray for grace

They surrounded me in full glory
Shared what they knew, gave what they had
Cleaned what needed to be cleaned
Gave water where there was thirst
They loved and protected what was precious in me
Nurtured my spirit and my mind
Repeatedly
Until I grew into a form of myself that warranted the respect
That I was forfeiting daily in my youthful ignorance

These wonderful women gave me shelter
Until my feet were grounded and steady
Until my wings were strong enough to lift me
When I needed to rise above my circumstances

Because of this
I pray for the opportunity to give
To be a vessel that shelters and supports
Loves and nurtures

And promotes growth
For my little sisters
That really just need
Someone to reach out
Someone to care enough to speak
Someone to love themselves enough to see themselves in them
To help them to prepare
For the day when they shall be spoken for

Black To Me

Check this out
I'm going to need you to come Black to me
To step in melanin laced power and meet me outside
I need you to come Black to me
so I can love you with all of this goodness that's the color of
the night

I want you to come so Black to me that we drip collard
greens and corn bread
I want you to hold on to me like your life depends on it, like
sagging pants in the hood trusting me to pull you up if start
to fall

I need you to come so Black to me that we smell like afro
sheen, shea butter and Egyptian musk incense
I'm so tired of us trying to assimilate and downplay the
magic of what makes us magical that I want to open hymn
books through telekinesis and replace police sirens with
negro spirituals

Let's embrace the cocoa coated essence that the whole
world tries daily to replicate- spends millions of dollars
trying to duplicate and let's be so Black that it hurts like a
slap in the mouth for talking during altar call at Little Galilee
of The Red Sea Over Jordan First Baptist AME- next door to
the liquor store, upstairs from the bakery on the corner of
14th and Malcolm X in everywhere Black USA

Come Black to me please- I want us to sweat gumbo and
saltine crackers, to need each other like the penny on the
needle of a skipping 45, I long for the reality of Geechee and
Gullah folklore and traditions shared during morning coffee
as truth, I want you to come so Black to me that we see
ourselves as Isis and Osiris, I want you to write your name
on my walls, so Black that we speak with the same tongue

and believe in one another again

I'm gonna love you Black to me so hard that we invoke
dancing ancestral shadows when we make love, so deep
that we reek of honey wine and jollof rice, so much that we
hear tribal drums in our sleep
I want you to come so Black to me that the stretch marks on
my thighs become a map to sacred treasures

Black like
Aretha Franklin blasting on Saturday morning meant your
mama was already up cleaning the whole house and you
can't go nowhere until it's all done- Black like wine coolers
made from $4.99 box wine and Seven-Up

Let the world see you come Black to me, see that we stand
together like two oak trees whose roots have intertwined,
let them see that we move like we belong together- steady
and strong- like we go way back- back like tuff skins and
green machines- back like high top fades and curly
ponytails, sweatsuits- the grey ones with the burgundy trim,
all white Nikes and Kangos

Come Black to me because I need you and you need me,
contrary to what's displayed as grossly misrepresented
truth, don't sweat that though- the lies they spread will be
the hell they live in
Come Black to me because we are the
superheroes that our babies need to see, because we are
the only ones that understand us, because this life is just
not the same without you
Come Black to me- so I can love you, so you can love me
Come Black to me so that we can be- love, be black love, so
that we can be Black- together-
I really miss you
Come Black to me

Praise Black Jesus, play Black Moses, give them flowers while they're still here Black roses...

D. Smoke

Possibly A Love Letter

I can't stop thinking about you and one day
Maybe this poem will be a love letter
So as far as love letters go
I guess it should begin with all of the usual things
About your eyes and your smile
Your laugh and your personality
How I feel when I see you
Or hear your voice
The tremors I get when you're close enough to touch me
But those things
As inexplicably resplendent as they are
Those things are not what stole my heart
I am in love with your mind
The quick wit and brilliance that oozes forth
Without concentrated effort is foreplay for me
Your desire and ability to search and destroy
Redefine and distribute information is bewitching
I love that you master words and turn everyday life situations
Into explosive thought-provoking food for the mind
You slay me regularly and I love it
I find myself more and more intrigued as our friendship grows
And sometimes all I want is for something you said
To be the last thing I heard before I went to sleep
Or the first thing I hear when I wake up
You are amazing
But because I am a hopeless romantic
Wired for fantasy and daydreams
And I don't want to scare you away
Or ruin a great friendship
I cannot share with you how I feel
I can only write poems
When I can't stop thinking about you
And hold onto the thought that if one day
if things should ever change
This poem
Will be a love letter

Poetry is when an emotion has found its thought, and the thought has found words.
– Robert Frost

No

We went to dinner
The fancy spot with no prices on the menu
He said he was going to take me places
I'd never been before
It got awkward when the waiter spoke to me
Welcome back, it's been a while since I've seen you
The room was silent when he asked the waiter
What kind of fish
is the Filet Mignon today?

Unpredictable, about to do something you've never done before...

Jamie Foxx

Public Service Announcement

If ya'll keep raising your daughters
And loving your sons
Don't get mad when somebody's daddy
Has to see your son
About his daughter

What If

He said being single wasn't that bad
But that he did miss toes touching in the bed
A warm body next to him
And
Coming home to someone

He also said that none of that was more important than his
peace
In that moment I thought, would he ever know
That I could be all of that for him?

Love in its essence, is spiritual fire -

Lucius Annaeus Seneca

Haiku #3

I wish that you knew
I hear what you do not say
And I love you too

Tales of a little Black girl #3

My mother insisted on buying me Black baby dolls when I
was a little girl because she wanted me to identify with
something that looked like me. When someone asked her
shouldn't I play with all types of dolls, her response was "Of
course she should, but she should learn to love herself first."
#Gospel

Birds flying high, you know how I feel...

Lauryn Hill & Nina Simone

Harvest Time

Southern trees bear a strange fruit
Blood on the leaves and blood at the root
Black bodies swinging in the southern breeze
Strange fruit hanging from the poplar trees."
Billie Holiday 1939

Strange fruit still being harvested
You don't have to go down south to get it
They be finding strange fruit everywhere
The harvesters have become masters at picking fresh crop
They like their fruit innocent, tender and unexpecting
They seem to prefer a random harvest of Black fruit
The kind that they need no reason to shoot

Black bodies be falling like leaves from Autumn trees
During a never -ending season of sorrow that darkens
dreams of tomorrow
Brothers leave home draped in prayers from their mamas
Who sit by the window, nervous at the ring of the phone
Unsure until the door opens again if their son will make it
home

People acting like we crazy for protesting
They aren't from the race of people who spent the last few
100 years
Digesting
Death
On a monthly, weekly and sometimes daily basis
They ain't felt the sting of constant slaps in their faces
If they're worried about their children not coming home
It's not out of fear of them being shot for holding a cell
phone
Or driving with a broken taillight, selling loosies or calling
for help

They don't worry that their children will be found dead with body parts missing in a jail cell.
They don't know what it feels like
to wake up to stories that make you feel like we're living in a corner of hell

Strange fruit crops falling dead in these streets
Must be something special for so many to try and get a piece
We march, we protest, we riot, and we scream
Trying to wake up from what we wish was a bad dream
They be hunting us now
Like rabbits in the snow
Still calling us niggers as they pull triggers
Cameras and cell phones on record
Makes no difference
Because were insignificant
And the person that died is the one gets tried
When the case goes to court
Defense attorneys with smear campaigns trying to make a victim look like a perpetrator
Dismissing the actions of badge wearing assassins emptying out clips like the terminator

Strange fruit getting picked so often and so quick
That we're almost desensitized
Numb from the hashtags
And the non- matter of Black lives
And when they're not killing us they're showing up ready for war
Pepper sprayed a Black girl who was upset and screaming for her daddy
She was only 9
9 being a number that must've been ringing strong
A police officer kept his knee on a neck for 9 minutes and 29 seconds
For a man who hadn't done anything wrong
Wrong being subjective because from a different perspective

When he woke up that morning, he was a Black man in a country that doesn't value Black lives and now his daughter has to survive being the descendant of strange fruit harvested in the street, murdered on camera for millions to see

Hands up, reaching for ID, standing in your grandmothers' backyard, kicked off a Bart train, asking for help in the rain, sitting in your own living room, walking or jogging down the street- then there's the one that's truly baffling- how do you get shot while you're at home asleep?
Strange fruit keeps falling and its Black lives that the harvest reaps
What must happen for it to be the last killing and it all stops
When will be the day that we won't have to leave home and wonder if today is the day that we'll be a part of a strange and bitter crop.

American trees bear a strange fruit
Blood on the leaves and blood at the root
Black bodies dying under American Breeze
Strange fruit rotting on Americas streets

The Gift

Black man
Have you ever had a woman love you so deeply
That when you made love to her, she kissed your soul?
Do you know what it feels like Black man
to have a woman open her legs
And her body calls out to you in silence?
Black man
Have you ever had a woman give herself so fully to you
that you were allowed access to her mind and heart through
her womb?
Do you know Black man
what it feels like for a woman to be hungry for you?
Black man
Have you ever had a woman receive you to the point that
your bodies became one?
Do you know what it feels like to align heartbeats and
breathing patterns in the middle of the night
or first thing in the morning in a full sweat that's intoxicating
Black man?
Have you ever had a woman speak love and life into your
ears while kissing them Black man?
Do you know Black man
what it feels like to be so consumed by a woman's passion
that her screams become a song you want to play on repeat?
Black man
Have you ever had a woman hypnotize you with the
movements of her body responding to the movements of
yours?
I wish I could help you to understand Black man
how very pure
How very sacred
How very precious
That treasure is
But unfortunately
I cannot make love to all of you

I write because there is a voice within me that will not be still.--
Sylvia Plath

Easy Prey

I am a hopeless romantic
I fall in love fast and hard with no breaks
It usually happens when I've decided that I won't do that
again
The butterflies from seeing a smile
Or hearing a voice
The heart pounding from a slight touch
The phone calls that last until the sun comes up with 15
minute intervals of silence
Spontaneous lunch dates, random gifts, an appreciation of the
same music
I'm an easy grab
I don't know how to not let you in
I don't have the wall that some women make you climb
I won't hold you accountable for what other people did to me
I'll spoil you without making you earn it and I will not use
you against you
So in the past my heart got broken a lot
Because I believed in people that didn't believe in themselves
I loved people that didn't love themselves
I supported people who had dreams but no ambition
I trusted people with my heart who were heartless

There were great friendships and amazing sex, lots of
laughter and mentally stimulating conversations but there
was always a moment
when the record skipped
When the record skipped
When the record skipped
It is at that moment
I was always aware
that this too would not last

The mistake was made, Love- slipped from my lips,
dripped down my chin and landed in his lap . . . .

Jill Scott

The Finest

He promised me the finest of everything
That's what he was used to
It was his standard
He kept his word
Colorless diamonds
Private jets
Chefs on my balcony for brunch
And plenty of crushed ice
To replenish the ice packs
For the finest black eye
That you could cover
With thousand-dollar shades

Dear White People

Dear White People
Please stop killing my husband. It's really way beyond out of control
Your behavior that is. The ease in which you seem to switch from
Present to murderous is quite alarming
Unsettling
It's already pushed me from sad, to hurt to angry to enraged to
Numb. I struggle with the apathy and the consistency.
I'm not sure that I can understand
Ever
Why you insist on the extinction of the Black Man.
Do you really love him so much that you don't want anyone else to have him?
Or do you really love him so much that you hate him because you love him?
Or do you really love him so much that you are in a constant state of maddening thoughts?
Or do you really love him so much that the thought of me loving him more drives you insane so
You would rather him dead than alive to be loved by me?

My Dear White People,
Please stop killing my Daddy.
What makes you hate my Daddy? So much that you want him dead?
Is it something that he said to you or was it something that he did?
Is it something like being the most desired on the planet
Or something about the power in his presence?
Or is it the fire in his eyes, the beauty in his smile or the glow of his sun kissed skin?
Do you really love him so much that you can't bear the thought of him being with his family?

Or do you really love him so much that you can't bear the
thought of him making more of him because
That would be too much for you?
Or do you love him so much that you hate him because you
love him?
Or do you love him so much that you would rather him dead
than alive to be loved by me?

My Dear, Dear, White People,
Please stop killing my sons.
I am unable to comprehend the pain from losing them.
Did they do something to you that makes you want to shoot
them?
With their hands up in the air
When they have no weapon
When they are sitting in a car
When they don't answer your questions quickly enough
When they are reaching for the identification that you asked
to see
When they are walking away from you unarmed
When they are in their own apartment watching television
What did they do to you that makes you want them dead?
Is it the promise of hope in their eyes?
Is it the possibility of them being the president one day?
Is their fear of your presence so intoxicating that you can't
help yourself?
Do you love them so much that you feel you have the right to
decide if they live or die?
Or do you love them so much that want to make sure that
nothing in this life ever harms them?
Or do you love them so much that you hate them because you
love them?
Or do you love them so much that you would rather them
dead than alive to be loved by me?

My Dear, Dear, Dear White People,
Please stop killing my Uncles

My Cousins, My Brothers
My best friend
And my Man.
What makes you lose control
Every single time that you encounter them?
What about them makes you so apathetic about their lives?
So pressured to put a cease to their existence?
So wounded upon sight that you defend yourself in a non-combative interaction?
Are you afraid that they see you for who you are?
Or that they know that you despise them so your shame takes over?
Are you worried that at the precise moment that they encounter you, that they might remember that they are warriors and align themselves to protect one another?
Are you terrified of the thought that they may not be afraid of you?
Does it bother you that they may not even give a damn about you?
That they may be more concerned about their families, their friends and their own lives?
Do you love them so much that you hate them?
That you hate the idea of them?
That you hate the idea of me loving them?
That you actually love hating them?
Is that where we are?
Is that what it is?
You love them so much
That you have lost your mind
That's what it is.
That is exactly what it is.
My Dearest White People
Please
Stop.

Poetry is a political act because it involves telling the truth. —
June Jordan

Sticks and Stones

Sticks and stones can break my bones, but words can never hurt me.
Liar.
Words hurt
They cut deep and slice
destroy and kill
All of the time
If you have managed to survive without being hurt by words then good for you
Bitch.
I spent several years of my adult life trying to erase and reprogram the tapes of words that split my self-esteem down the middle and then swallowed it whole
I see the product of verbally abusive environments every day struggling, fighting, floundering, and drowning in the seas of words that turned into violent Tsunamis that wiped out hope and regurgitated broken spirits into desolate bodies
Hoe

Anywhere, that you go, someone there has a deep wound festering and bleeding from the inside
that began with words spoken by someone else.
Words spoken from someone else that debilitated and devasted them at some point in their life.
Stupid

Words are power and they have wings. Once you give them flight you are responsible for the damage that they may do. You are accountable for the energy and the delivery that you set them forth with. You. It begins with you.
Trash

Be careful what you say to your children because they will believe you
They will identify, assimilate, and react in the fashion that

you chose to address them
Useless
Sorry
Weak
Bastard
Be mindful of how you speak to your man, your husband,
your brother and your son, he may have a high regard for you
and internalize your wrathful language as his truth
Broke
Ugly
Dumb
Lazy ass

Sticks and stones may break my bones, but names can never
hurt me
Faggot
Names are not just words
They are intertwined with identification
If names were not powerful then why
When we were stolen from our homeland
Then why
did they change them
From names that had honor and pride associated with them
I once read
"In the rush for humanity, they stole my name and left a
heritage by the wayside to die."

If names can never hurt you then why do you use them in
anger as a weapon
If names don't matter then why do we call them
Then why do we need them
Then why smile when someone calls you a Queen?
Why spend an hour in the mirror preparing for your day
Beautiful

Why go out your way for a stranger
Angel
Why
King

Because the truth is
that without words and names
words that become names
and names that are synonymous with words
You would never know how someone else sees you
You would also never know how to see yourself
When the interviewer says define yourself in 3 to 5 words
What would you say?
How do you answer that if your vocabulary has been
infiltrated with negative adjectives and adverbs?

Sticks and stones can break my bones, but words can never
hurt me.
Dummy
Words are all powerful
They have the potential to build or destroy
They can be used in a book to lead people to salvation
and they can also be used on a platform to lead people to war
For some cultures they are weapons of mass destruction,
especially ours
Nigga

So be careful
Don't abuse them
try not to misuse them
and never underestimate them.
Sticks and stones can break my bones
But words can never hurt me
Idiot

I plug in the mic, draw like a gunfight, I never use a cordless, or stand applaudless...

The Roots

Dope

Black women be so dope
everyone around them gets high off the fumes from their
essence
They be the kind of dope that you search for
That you feel like you can't live without
your heart is going to explode when you hit the right one
dope
Black women be uncut dope
Go out late night looking for it dope
no rest without them dope
change your name and all your life plans dope,
They be the high that you chase for the rest of your life
Naturally raised organic dope
No additives or derivatives necessary dope
Black women be so dope
all the women in the world spend their money and time trying
to be them
Lip injections and cheek implants
Tanning beds
 migrations to vacations where they lay on the beach and fry
themselves alive
Million-dollar industries thrive
Because of women that want to be the kind of dope that
Black women are
The kind of dope that stays on your mind
The kind of dope that you don't leave behind
The kind of dope that is so strong it fills you up
you forget what you were doing, and it don't matter
Because all you know is that you want and need more of that
More of that feeling that you can only get from a Black
woman
More of the lingering scent that you will only smell on a
Black woman
More of the intensity and fire that only a Black woman can
keep raging in you

All you know
Is that this is some good shit
That uncut primo that makes you feel like superman
You know you can do anything with some of that inside of
you
You'll do anything to get it
to keep it
to make sure that you never forget how it makes you feel
You'll chase that dope that be Black women forever
Because Black women
are the ultimate high

Tales of a little Black Girl #4

They all laughed at me on the playground when I said that Egyptians were Black. Then my highly insulted second grade teacher sent me to the principals' office when I spun the globe on her desk around and showed her Egypt sitting in the continent of Africa. It was my first experience of people not wanting to believe that royalty and greatness could originate from Africa. It was very confusing for me and it hurt my eight year old feelings.

Definitely a Love Letter

When you feel as if there is nothing left and nowhere to go
Please remember that I love you

When you are at your lowest and feel lost and defeated
Please remember that I am your safe place

I am not saying this lightly and every word in this poem I
hope you believe to be true
This is personal

I have seen you knocked down and trampled on
Disrespected and misunderstood
Belittled and shamed

I watch you move in a world that does not honor you
That loves to hate you
While you try to keep your head up
While you try to defy the odds of living past 25
While you try to be a great husband, father or friend
While you try to break the shackles of generational curses
And societal sub-par expectations

I watch and I see
What you go through
And I love you more because I see the God in you while the
world tries to dance with your demons

I love you because no one looks like you
No one smells like you
No one looks at me the way that you do
I love you from the top of your faded, dreadlocked, shaved,
curly, nappy ass head to the tips of your toes
I love the spread of your shoulders
The wind in your stride

I love that your presence can command a room and demand respect
Your hands over my womb calm storms from ancestral planes
You carry historical scars from trauma, pain, abuse and shame
On your back, yet you can still kiss my neck gently and make me feel alive
Your voice in my ear sends chills down my spine

You are incomparable and no misrepresentation of you can change my mind about you
I know that you are just as fragile as you are strong and that makes you even more beautiful to me
I love you for everything that you are, in your greatest hour and at your lowest point
I love you and I believe that you love me

So when you feel that there is nothing left and nowhere to go
Remember that I love you
When you feel lost and defeated
Remember that I am your safe place

When you need to scream allow me to make room for you
When you need to cry allow me to capture your tears with my heart
When you have been wounded allow me to comfort you in arms that will never let you go as long as you need them

Allow me to be the wings that society clipped from you
The smile that the justice system stripped from you
Please remember when you get frustrated with the world that you have someone who loves you from a holy place
Even if we've never met face to face
Remember Black man that I love you
I will always believe in and love you
And I will always believe that you love me too

Karma

It feels funny sometimes
Giving you advice on how to please and keep your wife
Mostly cause you didn't even try to let me love you
But there is a part of me that enjoys
You learning something
The hard way

Mama

Every day after my mama died
for a year
I
Waited
To
Die
too
The pain was stifling and blinding
I felt like a piece of me was missing
I kept looking for it
Trying to fill the hole
Until one morning
I looked in the mirror
And saw her face looking back at me
I looked at the rest of my body
And realized
That all of the pieces
Were still there

Exclamation Point

They say that when it's all over
your life is summed up by the dash between the date you
were born and the day that you died
I do not want my life to be contained in a dash
I want my life to be an undeniable exclamation point
I do not want
To be at the end of my life
thinking of all the things I could've, should've or would've
done if…
while giving someone who I'm leaving behind the advice to
do everything that they can

I want my life to be a scream so loud that non hearing people
stand at attention
I want to live so fully, so freely
that no one will ever be able to capture all of the things that
I've done
because they are immeasurable

I refuse to leave this place without turning my dash into an
exclamation point
I will be as much woman as is humanly possible, tuned into
my divine feminine power
Walking in the glory that I was gifted at birth; I will manifest
my own destiny

I am not afraid of the fear that tries to paralyze me when I'm
in unchartered territory
I am not ashamed when I have to start something over for the
one thousandth time
and I do not quit when things become uncomfortable
Because I,
I am a warrior
Because I,
I am a champion

I am a multi -faceted vessel put on this Earth, in this body
To have a full experience
I will not be deprived of that experience
especially by my own design

My dash will be an exclamation point
My exclamation point will be so bold,
so vivid
so exquisite
that when people see it they will have to stop what they're
doing and give it respect
It will have shoulders that carried, legs that danced, jewels
and skirts that move with the wind
My exclamation point will have a voice so strong that you
hear it wherever you are
It will be so magnificent that it humbles you and inspires a
salute
My life will never be summed up in a dash
Because I am a Queen
Because
I am the exemplar of being alive while living

Because
I am the walking embodiment of honoring your truth
And living it
And as the multi-faceted vessel put on this Earth in this body
To have a full experience
By my design
My dash will be
An undeniable, boldly italicized exclamation point

You can win, as long as you keep your head to the sky. . . .

The Sounds of Blackness

Haiku #4

Open your mouth wide
Taste the beauty of your dreams
Then spit them all out

Friend Zone

He friend zoned me ya'll
Amazing, black, warrior masterpiece of a man
That I finally had the chance to get to know
We talk about everything and laugh
A lot,
He is everything I thought he would be
With the addition of a few pleasant surprises
And I was excited that if we really start to know each other
A concept long played out in my head might just be right
But then he friend zoned me

I wondered if he knew that the heaven I see in his eyes
Could always be obtainable if he was locked between my thighs
That my heart skips a beat every time I hear his voice
That for me he is absolutely the perfect choice
That I want to kiss his forehead and the tip of his nose
But I respect his friend zone
Because this time I don't want to choose
I need to be chose
I wonder sometimes if he knows
That I am everything that he ever imagined love to be
That I am the perfect verse
Over a tight ass beat
Sometimes when we share it gets real deep
Sometimes I see his face and say his name before I fall asleep

We can agree to disagree, and he laughs at my jokes
We have similar morals and values,
My grandmama used to say you've got be equally yoked
And we are
So I find myself enjoying him fully only in my mind
Freely loving every inch of him
In my own world and on my own time
It doesn't stop me from being a great friend

Because I didn't take a loss
He's a great friend also so he's
Kinda
Mine

I still think things that I cannot say
I still hold out
that maybe
one day
But I'm chill and I can handle it
It's not hard and it doesn't hurt
I just know that if we stepped into it together
This shit would really work

So I just fall back and stay in my place
Thinking while I'm drinking
about his beautiful face
Smiling while licking my ice cream
Knowing he probably tastes just like the chocolate in this
cone

It's just a nice nasty thought though
Because
I'm in the friend zone

Fast Forward

Unnecessary idle chatter
Circles of conversation
About things that don't matter

Time wasted

Trying to not get toasted
Wheels spinning
Nights getting shorter

Let's cut the bullshit and fast forward to the seduction

I'm not in need of sweet nothings
Never been interested in
Untouchable fantasies
Or
Impossible daydreams
Mindless shopping sprees
Exhausting vacations
Or
Promises that probably won't be kept

I'm here because I'm feeling you
So we can just
Cut the bullshit
And fast forward to the seduction

You don't have to try to woo me
Convince me
Or prove anything
Those are measures that won't gain ground for you

You can really
Cut the bullshit
And fast forward to the seduction

Get busy
With the neck kissing and lip sucking
Find somewhere soft on me that you like
And put your hands all over it
Get as close as you can
And breathe on me
A little bit
Nibble a little
Bite a little
Pull my hair a little
And make love to me with your eyes
Relax my mind
With the weight of your body on mine

I hope that by now
By the time that I finish this poem
You realize that we never need
To waste precious moments
Waiting for
The right moment
We can always
Cut the bullshit
And
Fast forward to the seduction

Every secret of a writer's soul, every experience of his life, every quality of his mind, is written large in his works. – Virginia Woolf

Reckless

I left them in pieces
I traded
Niggas ain't shit stories with girlfriends
I picked and plucked them at random
Spoiled and fucked them into fandom
Then when my cup was full
From having to respond to them
I would just
Disappear
Move on to the next
Fine ass muthafuka
That was smiling at me
Like he was hungry
It was easy to do them
You know
How they do us
Until that one day
When I saw a deep pain
In the eyes of someone I'd ghosted
And he was struggling
With the sight of me
Tears rimmed in his eyes
And he couldn't even speak
At that moment
I knew that I had become
One of those niggas
That wasn't shit

One day, all them bags, gone get in your way. . .

Erykah Badu

I hate this place

I hate this place. Hate is a strong word but, in some instances, it isn't strong enough because I can't begin to stress to you enough that I hate this place. This place being a mindset as much as a geographical pinpoint. I keep hoping that I'll wake up and find that Black Panther wasn't a dream so that I can buy a one -way ticket to Wakanda.

This place where Black women hate other Black women, hate Black men and hate themselves so much that they cut, clip and snip themselves into distorted Black Barbies
This place where Black men hate other Black men, hate Black women and hate themselves so much that they kill each other over shoes, money that they didn't earn and what a motherfucka said

This place where an endless catch 22 has one fucked up individual dating another damaged individual and they spend all of their time blaming each other for why they're so fucked up

I hate this place
This place where we are at constant war with a socio-economic construct, generational curses, the government, the police and ourselves.
This place where reality shows glorify betrayal, deceit and dysfunction in thousand -dollar shoes, with perfect makeup and hair fighting over somebody else's man.
This place where women think selling pussy is a career move and men think that gorilla pimping 15- and 16-year-old girls is a justifiable source of income.

This place is so crazy that a release of the same pair of Jordans from twenty years ago causes mob mentality.
Songs about pharmaceutical drugs go platinum and cartoons have funerals in them.

Easter lilies are blooming in January, and Spring sometimes just decides to sit a season out.
Laws are changed due to cruelty to animals but it's un-American to protest the killing of innocent people.

I tell you
I hate it here
Teachers and preachers molesting children, 35-year-old parents getting high with their kids, Becky got 911 on speed dial and
There's a deadly virus that can be transmitted by touch and people are still videotaping parties with no masks, passing drinks, blunts and plates.

I want a one- way ticket to Wakanda
Where everybody is fly
No one is ostracized for being or looking different
You can be immersed in the purple stuff and take a spiritual journey and get guidance from your ancestors
The weather is always nice, people sing and dance in harmony and unison
And there's an element there that can heal your injuries and cure all illnesses
Where your Blackness doesn't put a target on your back
It emphasizes your power
You can't go wrong in a place that's built for wholeness and love
And every day that I wake up and see what's going on in this country, I get a little upset that Wakanda is not real
Because I hate it here

I hate it here but what's happening here pales in comparison to some other places. I could go somewhere else and be subject to their insanity and the horrors that people live with daily in countries where there is no democracy. Where people live in a state of war or the possibility of one at any moment. I could hide in my house and create a perfectly beautiful comfortable sanctuary; I could just hit the road and travel to places that only make me feel good. But it wouldn't change the tangible energy that threatens my peace of mind. It might make a temporary difference, but it wouldn't change anything.

All I want to do is wake up one day and everything is different
Everything is just, fair and respectable
I want to live in a country that's deemed the greatest on the planet, amongst my own people
And not hate it here

Tales of a little Black Girl #5

The first time that I was called a "troublemaker", I was five years old. Excitedly entering my kindergarten classroom, everyone was told to hang their jackets up on the hook by their name. I told the teacher that I didn't see my name. She pointed to a hook that spelled my name with a K. I told her that's not my name. She told me that it was, and it means the same thing.

I carried my jacket all day. When my mother came to pick me up from school, the teacher said "We have a small problem, Carla is being a bit of a troublemaker. She refused to hang her coat up by her name." My mama looked at me and I pointed to the name tag by the coat hook that spelled my name with a K. She then turned to the teacher and said "That is not her name. The only problem here is that you had a power play with a five-year-old instead of just changing a K to a C. The bigger problem, however, is that you don't seem to understand the damage that you do- especially to children of color, when you diminish and dismiss their right to their true name." And then she took my hand and said, "Let's go, tomorrow, your name will be above the coat hook."

That was the first time I remember falling in love with my mama, and deciding that when I grew up, I would be just like her.

Him

We traveled all of the time
I really liked him
Kinda
20 years my senior
Established and refined
He knew how to make you feel
Special
So it was a little awkward
The day that I put my size 8,
Chocolate, toned up self into a bikini
And got into the hot tub
He was walking over to join me and said
"You've got a nice body,
 don't ever let yourself go."
And I looked up from the hot, bubbling water at him
Standing over me
About 6 months pregnant with twins
And hairs coming out of his nose
And I fell out laughing

Don't it always seem to go, that you don't know what you've got til it's gone...

Janet Jackson

Her

She was little in the waist and cute in the face
All cultured and classy
Smelling like incense and lavender
She had a beautiful smile
All about crystals and manifestations
Truth telling and empowerment
Then I watched her betray her best friend
Disrespect her mother
And
Deliberately deceive and almost destroy
Her daughter
When we broke up
she said that I broke her heart
I told her
I didn't know you had one

Words have no power to impress the mind without the exquisite horror of their reality.
-- Edgar Allen Poe

Haiku #5

Forever seems short
When days die at dusk
And life starts to fade

Remember

There was a time when your shadow was my friend
It meant that you were somewhere near
Close enough to protect me
To
Evaluate the purpose of my presence
You
Were always watching
Together we built kingdoms
We created legacies
We crossed many lands
Hand in hand
Side by side
Moving as one
You were always there
And I remember you

We ran by night
Silently
Fearlessly
Barefoot
Heavy in heart and strong in spirit
Within arm's reach always
We missed not a step-in unison
We swallowed screams and tears

They
Opened and Oak tree up on your back
And you still carried me
When my body betrayed my will
Strong and mighty
You were always there
And I remember you

Drenched, dazed and weary
We sang

We marched
We made love
Under trees with blood-soaked roots

Together we brought the entire world to its feet
To attention
As we made historical moves
That created pathways for unborn children
Even when you were away
You were always there
And I
I remember you

Somewhere along the way
We were separated
Transfused with foreign realities
Placed on different planes and paths
We began
To spiritually dismember one another
To annihilate the present wonders of who we were
To one another

There are many tears that tell our story
Many sands that held our footprints
Many miracles that bore our signature
That bore fruit because we once covered
Created and recreated one another
Diligently
Unceasingly

When I have the pleasure
Of encountering you now
As you pass me by on the street
I am moved to silence at times
Quickly stilled and overwhelmed
By the knowing
Without physical recognition

A never-ending inferno of love
Has transcended time
And enveloped the very moment
That we beheld one another again

You
Have another name that does not suit you
But your eyes give flight to your spirit
And I can still smell you in the morning air
Taste the salt of your sweat on my lips
I can still feel you inside of me
Your handprints
Are seared into the blueprints of my thighs
Forever

As you pass me by with the same smile and a brief hello
I levitate
I relax into your descending silhouette
Dancing in my mind with you again
Cheek to cheek
Breast to breast
Hip to hip
Presence to presence
I am satiated by the man that I know you are
And I
I remember you

I would rather share one lifetime with you than face all the ages of this world alone. — J.R.R. Tolkien

This is Why I Spit

Fractured pieces of historical monuments
Travel with their pants hanging around their knees
Making what was once a powerful stride
Resemble a slaves shackled shuffle
This Is why I spit

Confused masses of phenomenal masterpieces
Present themselves daily
Without regard for regality
Sun kissed clones in droves
Wearing cloaks of self- hatred and mediocrity
This is why I spit

Juvenile heirs to greatness
Suffer from nothing resembling greatness to witness
So they send out smoke signals of distress
As they try to understand the mess that bears no significance
But is in mass abundance
They beg for attention in selfless bliss
Beg for acceptance
Through a drug induced kiss
This is why
I spit this shit

I spit and can't quit because the words in my head
Form pictures that will make you sick
Self-inflicted wounds on my people as a whole
Fester and bleed
From a lack of self
Con- trol

Roll a few
Drink a few
Think not
And kill a few

Do some time behind literal or psychological bars
Have a barbecue for getting out of the pen
Have a party for getting pregnant
Again
And again
And again

Reward your children for going to school for a whole week
Buy a new car because you qualified for section 8
And your stamps increased
Teach your pre- teen son to use a gun
Show your teenage daughter
How to let other bitches know
That she ain't the one
This is why I spit this shit

For the nonsense and madness that I can't digest
For the five funerals in three weeks
When I couldn't damn sleep
Unnatural obsessions
Supernatural progression of
Genocide

White collar lynch mobs
That choke you to death
With the stroke of a pen
Rope is now obsolete
Brain tumors develop in your sleep
Grown women wearing pajamas as a fashion statement
This is where it begins to get deep
And this is why
I spit this shit

I spit because there's a bad taste in my mouth
I spit because I can't hold the truth hostage
I spit so I can cocoon myself
In reality and the colors of life

I spit so people with no vision
Can hear what it looks like
Can feel what it sounds like
Can see what it's really not like

So they can understand
That it all has a heartbeat
Not unlike my own
This is why I spit

So I don't fall into an artistic abyss
And be completely amiss
Like the girls on the corner
Who'll sell you a kiss

Like the boys who ride or die
Ride to die
And their last words are a diss

Too many of my people leave here early to go home
I'm tired of I won't complain
As the standard for a young man's funeral song

That's why I worry not about the foolishness
Of trying to be the next hit
The world gives me enough quakes and rhythms to keep
writing
And that is why
I spit this shit

The Poem About Joy

In the midst of a pandemic,
Having to wear masks, be sheltered in place and
Basically, survive primarily off of virtual interactions
I wanted to write a poem about joy
Something that would make people remember
Why life is so beautiful
I wanted to sit down and just write a poem about joy
but then I thought
About the families of Daunte Wright, Rayshad Brooks,
Daniel Prude, George Floyd, Breonna Taylor and Atiana
Jefferson

So, I changed my focus to just possibly providing a reason to
smile
and then I thought about the friends of Aura Rosser, Stephon
Clark, Botham Jean, Philando Castille, Alton Sterling,
Freddie Gray, Janisha Fonville and Eric Garner

Then I thought, maybe Joy is pushing it during such trying
times and That I should just try to get a piece done about
gratitude

So, I sat down to write my poem that changed from, joy, to
smiles, to gratitude

and my head was flooded with the possible legacies now
cancelled of Michelle Casseaus, Akai Gurley, Gabriella
Nevarez, Tamir Rice, Michael Brown, Tanisha Anderson,
Matthew Williams and James Lionel Johnson

A poem about something joyful could really make a
difference in our lives right now and I really wanted to write
one, but one police officer was found guilty of murder the

other day and I thought about how many others will never be tried as the graves hold silent screams from Dominique Williams, Marvin Scott, Jenoah Donald, Patrick Warren, Xzavier Hill, Robert Howard, Vincent Belmonte and Bennie Edwards

So, I struggled

With my dictionary of synonyms and antonyms handy by my keyboard to find the words to write a poem about joy

I struggle finding the light at the end of the tunnel, the ever-elusive pot of gold at the end of the rainbow as I think about Casey Goodson Jr., Aiden Ellison, Quavan Charles, Kevin Peterson Jr., Walter Wallace Jr., Jonathan Price, Kurt Reinhold, Dyon Kizzoe and Damian Daniels

It's beginning to hurt, this effort that I'm making to write a poem about joy during a time when I know there are mothers, fathers, brothers, sisters and children who can't sleep at night peacefully as they mourn the losses of Anthony McClain, Julian laws, Maurice Wagner, Priscilla Stater, Robert Forbes, Kaniel Flowers, Jamal Floyd and James Scurlock

But, the impact of a poem about joy during times like these is so important and necessary that I continue writing and searching, now more so hoping that something triggers joyful thoughts and experiences seeking a home through a poem but I know that there are people who will never experience joy again because a piece of them died with Calvin Horton Jr., Tony McDade, Dion Johnson, Maurice Gordon, Cornelius Frederico, Steven Taylor and Barry Gedeus,. I know that Manuel Ellis, Ahmaud Arberry, Lionel Morris, Jaquyn O'Neill Light, William Greer, Jarvis Tarver, Miciah Lee, John Neville and Michael Dean along with Byron Williams, Elijah McClain, Jaleel Medlock, Titi Gulley, Dominique Clayton, Pamela Turner, Ronald Greene, Sterling Higgins,

Bradley Blackshire, Jasmine McBride and Makiah Bryant all will never have the opportunity to live, love and breathe again. I want to continue writing this. piece that was supposed to be about joy, but the list of names is so long that I have don't think that I have the words or enough tears

So, I have to end this poem the same way that I started it. Wanting to write a poem about joy, something that would make people remember why life

Is so beautiful

Just Fucking

I tried to love you
But our relationship kept getting in the way
We kept laughing and sharing
Growing and enjoying
But
You were damaged and I was broken
So the reasons we held on so tightly
We're the wrong reasons for that particular season
And when the kisses became love making
We were consumed by a fire that smothered memories of
pain
But left flood gates open for visitation
There is a pillow that still holds screams
Muffled from face down release in total submission
A wall that held silhouettes of legs spread east and west
A purple plush towel that never quite finished drying my
body because
Round two was always a few moments away
And a neighbor downstairs in 127 who was always polite but
could never look at me directly without turning dark red
I remember that
And how hard I was trying to love you
But our relationship kept getting in the way
Every time I thought we were becoming closer
We made more maddening love and the you that knew only
my body
Was the only you I fully knew
You blocked me
At every turn
Pushed me back while pulling me in
You made sure that I couldn't get close enough to connect
To make you feel
To love you from a sacred place

And I did the dance for as long as I could
Until the day that I'd been dreading came along
The day that I had to ask what are we doing
Your response was simple, straight to the point
And it freed me,
Gave me permission to let go
So that I could let go
It was much easier than I thought
After being so mesmerized by your eyes
Held hostage by the scent you left in my sheets
After spending endless days laughing until we cried
Driving just to see the sun rise or set without an obstructed
view
Timeless moments where there were tears without questions
and
Words were unnecessary
We actually played strip scrabble
I mean who does that
Amongst so many other things
We did so much while I was trying to love you
And our relationship kept getting in the way
Must have been Oshun
Protecting me
Because a year became a blurred moment
when your answer to my question was
We

Are

Just fucking

I'm in need of love, and you're need of love, so what about us?

Jodeci

Untitled

Sometimes

I lay out in the backyard

naked

And

let

the

moon

eat

me

out

Transition of Power

I thought I had protected myself

Kept the softness hidden

Tucked away sweetly, deeply

Just wanted to make sure that no one could just walk up

And take it

You know how they do,

See a weak spot, manipulate it and make it theirs

Then sooner

Or later

You find yourself being devoured

Because you let too much be seen

Felt

Heard too soon

Your essence dripping like honey from fangs that have bitten

Into a honeycomb

Because you didn't protect yourself

I'm tired of having to protect myself

Of camouflaging the gentility that I'd rather be my first face

All I want

Is to let that sweetness rise to the top

And sit there for a little while

I'd like to be vulnerable and exposed without fear

Of intrusion or injury

Seemed like quite a feat so I stopped

And just when I thought that maybe

I could just let it be what it is

because

No one knew what was under the cover

That I was not going to be rendered powerless by exposure

Somebody saw me

Somebody saw me naked and found it amusing

that I saw my sweetness

As a weakness

He said it was beautiful

And he called it

Kryptonite

To gain your own voice, you have to forget
about having it heard. —
Allen Ginsberg

Wonder

Every time I see you my stomach drops a little.

I try to keep my eyes from staring at your lips or looking directly into yours because,

you make me weak.

 I would like to know what it would feel like if your hands were perfectly positioned on my thighs and hips in the dark. I would like to know if your kiss is as good as your conversation, because you seem,

you seem to get me.

I sometimes think about you taking control of me and making me do

what I want to do anyway.

Every time I see you my stomach drops a little.

But I just take a deep breath, smile and engage in casual friendly conversation because we both belong to someone else. So, I interact with respect, integrity and grace and just enjoy our chat.

But still, I wonder.

This is the highest cost, take you and make you off...

Maxwell

Time

Time

Does not stop, wait or make promises

But as long as I have breath in my body

I will have time for you

I will not take advantage of the time that you share with me

I will not forget the time that we spent building what we have

I will honor the time that we used to hold conversations about people,

God and constellations

I will not betray the times that we walked on tears trying to hold one another up

I will not forget the times that you helped me get closer to my dreams

I will not lose track of time and make you wait for anything

I will always have time for you

Time to laugh

And time to cry

Time to allow you to grow and time to let you know

That my heart and mind are precious gifts, but they are nothing

Without time

I will not abuse the trust that you extended during the times you shared your fears and pain

I will never use you against you when I get angry

I will take the time to massage your feet when you're tired and your mind when you're confused

I will make sure that I always have time to hear you and even more time to listen

I will not let time pass without saying I love you

Or showing you how much

Because time

Time does not stop, wait or make promises

But as long as I have breath in my body

I will have time for you

Enough time to make sure that you're smiling

Enough time to make sure that I am never a question

Enough time to make you feel as if there is enough time

Haiku #6

They call me a Queen

While they trample on my crown

So, who believes it

Tadow

Masego & FKJ

Imperfectly Perfect

This poem is for the women whose thighs have been kissed by lightning
The women who don't look like any of what you see on IG
The beautiful women with flat feet and wide hips that make a dress beg for mercy
The under rated and unappreciated women who like the gap between their front teeth, the women with tiger stripes on their wombs who grace their waists with beads and wear anklets and toe rings on well-greased calloused feet

This is for the women who don't advertise bedroom skills or brag about their pussies, the women who love deeply and fiercely, who aren't afraid to cry, apologize or humble themselves because they understand their power. The warrior women and rememberers who see signs in the stars and the clouds, the women who listen when the wind speaks and dance in the rain, the women who speak their truth and own it

The women who look in the mirror and check themselves from the inside first. The women who don't compare themselves to other women or gage their worth by what they don't have
This is for the women who wear feathers and flowers in their hair, who have freckles perfectly placed, high cheekbones, full lips and walk with a switch that mesmerizes passersby. The women who speak life and beauty into the ears of people who listen and plant seeds that will bear fruit into the hearts of people who don't

This poem
Is for the women who aren't afraid to be afraid and who push through the fear, the healers and the teachers who touch the souls of everyone that they meet, this poem is for the women who have razor blades for tongues that are carefully kept and

can destroy you
The women who respect their elders, love their children and
represent at all times
The women who start and take no shit, who make full meals
from three ingredients and sing while taking a bath or
walking down the street

This poem is for
The women who have band aids on their hearts and fire in
their eyes because they've been burned one time too many,
the women who haven't let the deep cuts of betrayal and
deceit rob them of their naturally sweet essence and who
continue loving freely
The women who always have something for you to eat
whether it be physically or mentally, the women who can
give you a hug and you forget what was bothering you
The queen mother women who mentor, groom, educate and
inspire you, the women who enter a room and people start
adjusting themselves
The misunderstood, underestimated, second guessed and
dismissed women who talk and laugh loud, wear whatever
they want and don't give a damn what you think
This poem is for all of you
And it is a quite simple piece
Stand up Queen
I see you
I salute you
And I love you

for being you

Hold fast to dreams, for if dreams die, life is a broken winged bird, that cannot fly.---
Langston Hughes

Where is My Parade

Where is my parade? My hashtag, my t-shirt
I am the best thing since sliced bread you know.
The envy of all women, the desire of all men,
The conduit for life, the ultimate warrior
the praying, loving, caring, nurturing, forgiving,
unconditionally incredible
reason why you have survived

I am the truth

Where is my salute.
My fireworks and a soul stirring solo
I'd appreciate my flowers and a crown too
How about one of those presidential plaques
a fancy ink pen and a watch with a nice inscription
I would like to know where is my stuff
You know, the type of things that you are supposed to give
to prestigious people
Let alone someone as important as me-
Did you forget that I loved you so much
I have spent centuries trying to restore you
To rebuild and replenish you?
Have I mentioned that I carried your children and
Whether you chose to stay or not- I loved them
I even named one after you, didn't matter that the youngest is
the one with your eyes
Because for me loving them meant loving you more
If that's at all possible

It's not easy being the ship , the ocean and the storm-
To be the Sun and the stars
A pillow, blanket, comforter and bed all in one

To be everything for everyone and still have the strength to
be enough for myself
To be all things and keep smiling- that alone is quite
impressive

Can you imagine
the joy that lives between my legs
Causes quite a commotion sometimes
There is a song in my smile,
a refuge in my eyes, a safe harbor between these 38 D's,
there is a symphony in my stride
Why do you think the people stare?
trying to see where that glorious sound is emanating from
Can't even help it
At my weakest and lowest I led a nation
never mind that was after seeing you slaughtered
I stood then and still do
Patiently waiting
for my cake so I can eat it too
For sure I'm going to
without a fork
Tastes better out of my hands
Are you listening
I asked you a question

Where is my VIP pass, Carte blanch first class everything
I don't ask for much but I definitely deserve it
Much that is
The front row, the escort, the complimentary champagne and
the nod from the featured guests
Sit me at the head of that table
I have been for so long I'd be uncomfortable elsewhere
Where is the respect?
The foot and back rubs, the fluffy white robe and those house
slippers that I can't find anywhere with the extra cushion

around the toes
Bring some of those fancy chocolates with the sea salt and
red pepper flakes
Who'd ever thought you could add my tears to candy and
have a delightful treat?
Don't dare leave out the champagne, candles, incense, and a
mango
they are critical for ambiance and comfort
You haven't answered my question
Where is my stuff?
And I want it all
You keep acting like you forgot who I am
I am every woman, everywhere
I am you while being your reason for living
I am the truth
I am your truth
Oh Please believe it

In the meantime

I'm still waiting for my stuff

Write what should not be forgotten. — Isabel Allende

Where is My Parade? – Spoken Word – Full Album-

Carla J. Lawson "Isis the Poet"

About The Author

Carla J. Lawson is a Bay Area, California-bred poet/author/visual artist.

Her other published works include a sci-fi/afro-futurism trilogy with an African American female protagonist called "Odara's Rise". The trilogy includes "The Return", "The Weavers", and "The Decision". All of her literary work can be found on her literary website- www.carlajlawson.com

They can also be found on Amazon and Barnes and Noble online. Carla's visual art can be found at https://carla-js-art.square.site

IG - @isisthepoet

IG - @Carlajsart

Twitter - @isisthepoet

#isisthepoet #iammscarla

Ingram Content Group UK Ltd.
Milton Keynes UK
UKHW051952270323
419219UK00010B/77